AF211952

LALLIE TIDWEL

PRACTICAL WEDDING

The Ultimate Guide to Planning a Practical Wedding, Learn The Best Tips and Strategies on How to Organize a Beautiful Wedding on a Budget

Descrierea CIP a Bibliotecii Naţionale a României
LALLIE TIDWEL
   PRACTICAL WEDDING. The Ultimate Guide to Planning a Practical Wedding, Learn The Best Tips and Strategies on How to Organize a Beautiful Wedding on a Budget / Lallie Tidwel – Bucharest: Editura My Ebook, 2021
   ISBN

LALLIE TIDWEL

PRACTICAL WEDDING

The Ultimate Guide to Planning a Practical Wedding, Learn The Best Tips and Strategies on How to Organize a Beautiful Wedding on a Budget

My Ebook Publishing House
Bucharest, 2021

TABLE OF CONTENTS

INTRODUCTION

He's popped the question. The ring is on your finger.

Now comes the stressful part. You want to throw the wedding of your dreams, but you're not Donald Trump's kid. What do you do?

Statistics say the average wedding costs $20,000.

Most young girls dream of the fairy tale wedding: long white gown, 8 bridesmaids, a sit-down dinner, the band everyone dances to.

Many brides have been dreaming about their wedding day since childhood. These dreams come with an expensive price tag and the realization of their fairytale day may be distant. Although weddings are very costly today, your dream day can happen. I am going to share some tips to cut corners and save money without making huge sacrifices.

By taking the time to plan and investigate, you will be amazed at the amount of money that you save. Would you arrive at an interview for your dream job without prior preparation? No, you would not and that is why preparation and research will make your wedding a success without re- mortgaging the house!

It's only natural to want the Cinderella fantasy wedding, complete with ice sculptures, a heavenly cake, and thousands of guests who've flown in from around the world to enjoy the accompanying dinner. It's only human to cry at the bill that this dream can rack up.

Costs can add up quickly. Factor in the meal, the liquor, the music, the dress, the flowers, the photographer, the decorations and the dream wedding can seem way out of your league. But it doesn't have to be.

How can the average person have a beautiful wedding with all the bells and whistles on a working person's salary? Perhaps the three letters/words that say it best are – DIY (do it yourself!)

Spending your life savings on your big day is crazy. You can have elegant, beautiful weddings without breaking the bank.

Having a cheap wedding doesn't mean giving up style or sentimentality. It means using your imagination, using your own hands or the help of friends and family. Ask anyone you know to help out. Almost everyone will be happy to oblige. They'll be part of your special day which makes them special as well!

This book will give you the best tips and tricks from the experts to cut costs without cutting class and sophistication. No one will know that your budget equals the grocery bill of a family of 4. They'll be oblivious as they toast the new couple and enjoy a party to put all other party's to shame!

We'll explore ways to save on all aspects of your wedding. Don't think you have to give up anything because it can all be covered. All it takes is the cooperation of your family and friends coupled with a little positive self-talk and perseverance.

I have been married twice (don't worry, I got it right the second time!) For both of my weddings, I had amazing ceremonies and receptions for around $2,000. They were the talk of the town both now and then. Throughout this book, I will tell you what we did to save money and still have an amazing wedding/reception. Hopefully, you can gain some insight into a dream event for not a lot of money - just like we had!

Let us show you how to throw a dream wedding on a shoestring budget!

WHERE TO START?

There's so much to do, it can be mind-numbing. Don't worry. I planned and held my first wedding in two months and my second wedding in three months. If you have the luxury of a year or more, feel lucky!

We'll provide you with a wedding planner at the end of this book for you to keep with you as you plan your dream wedding. Planning is essential, so our checklist could be your best friend! You may want to invest in a cheap folder to keep all of your notes in order. Print out the checklists at the end of this book and keep them in that folder along with any receipts and/or quotes that you get!

You need to decide who will pay for the wedding. The typical wedding planner dictates that the bride's parents pay for the wedding. In reality, these days that isn't always the norm.

My second husband and I both have two sets of parent.

We had been living together for 8 years, but were ill equipped to throw our own wedding. We could contribute, sure, but to throw the whole shin-dig would be out of our realm. We asked each parent-couple to contribute $500 and they all agreed wholeheartedly. That gave us a budget of $2,000 which was plenty!

We're assuming you want a traditional ceremony as opposed to a "theme" wedding. That information alone could compose a whole other e-book. Assuming you want a traditional wedding, the first decisions to be made include: the date, your attendants, and where the reception will be held. Of course, the date might be your most important decision.

Traditionally, couples tie the knot on a Saturday. If you really want to save some cash, consider having your ceremony on a Thursday or Friday. How about having a

Sunday service on a holiday weekend? You'll find that there are many more open dates on these days and you'll ultimately realize more savings by booking on these less traditional time frames. Many reception locations will offer a discount for an off day. If they don t offer it, ask for it.

Also, you may want to consider an early marriage and an early reception. An 11:00 marriage with a reception immediately following can realize great savings as most guests will have
12

already had lunch before your ceremony and the reception will most likely be over by dinner, so all you'll have to provide is some light finger foods to tide over those rumbling tummies!

Additional savings may be realized by having your wedding in the months of November through April. These months are less busy for most wedding related services and locations. Again, ask for a discount for being off-season.

You need to decide how many attendants you will have so you can bestow the honor on them early enough! They can save the date and help you plan! Traditionally, the bridesmaids are responsible for their own wedding attire, but the bride usually has the final say on what they wear. Be mindful of your attendants' financial situation and don't choose that $500 satin chiffon number. Remember, you're trying to throw a wedding on a budget. Let them save some cash as well! We'll have some suggestions later on in this book for attendant attire, so keep that in the back of your mind!

Where your reception will be held is another huge decision that has to be made early on in the wedding planning stage. If you want to opt for a traditional reception hall, you'll have to book early to be sure you can get the venue of your choice.

If you or someone in your family is the member of a benevolent association (The Elks, The Moose, The American

Legion), consider these as viable options. They often give discounts to members and you will probably have access to a huge area for your wedding reception as opposed to Aunt Emily's backyard! Just remember to book early!

With my first wedding, we married on a Saturday and held our reception in the church parish hall. It was a Catholic church and they graciously allowed us the ultimate leniency with liquor, food, etc. Since we were members of the church, we only paid $50 to rent it for the afternoon.

My second husband and I chose to be married on a Saturday at our local church and held the reception at the local American Legion where both my (future) husband and my father were members. We saved a ton by booking the Legion the day after my husband and I decided to marry.

Plus, we saved on the headache of trying to find a reception hall!

We'll have much more on the dream reception later in this book, but remember to book early. Having that out of the way will free up more of your time to concentrate on the little details that can mean so much!

You can also look to find a free place to hold your reception such as a friend's home, a church's reception hall, or even the local fire department's reception hall! You could look into a local park, art gallery, and even your own home.

You'll need to start on a guest list as soon as possible and begin thinking about invitations.

YOU ARE CORDIALLY INVITED...

Ideally, invitations should be mailed out 6-8 weeks before the big day to give guests time to make arrangements to attend and RSVP back to you.

The first step is to get organized. Remember when we suggested a folder earlier? This is where it comes in especially handy! Begin by making a list of the people you just can't stand to get married without them there. This will probably be mostly relatives and close friends. Ask your parents and the groom's parents to provide you with a list of who they would like to invite. Make sure you have accurate addresses for your guests.

One caution here: don't think you HAVE to invite everyone you know. If you haven't talked to your high school lab partner since graduation, he or she probably doesn't need to be invited. And don't get all caught up in possibly offending someone by not inviting them to your wedding.

Often, people get sick of attending weddings for people they barely know. Unless you talk to them every day, chances are pretty good that they won't give it a second thought when your invitation doesn't arrive. Remember, you're trying to save some money on your big day. Extra people means extra expense – cut corners here.

Once you have your guest list, you'll have an idea of how many invitations you'll need. Next, you'll need to pick a design.

Wedding invitations shouldn't be a big expense for you. Yes, when it's delivered all pretty in its customized envelope and small tissue square inside, it can make an impression – for about a minute! Most people read it once, note the date, take out the RSVP card and throw the invite away. So why spend a lot on them? Remember, we're trying to save money here!

The obvious thing to do with your invites is to create them yourself on your personal computer. You can use Microsoft Word or Publisher to create beautiful invitations that are ALL you!

There also are inexpensive programs out there specifically made for creating invitations and greeting cards. The best part about buying programs like this is being able to use it again after the wedding is over! I've had this program save me many times to print out a special occasion card (Birthday, Anniversary) at the last minute if I've forgotten!

You can buy heavy card stock at any office supply or discount store. Consider some pre-printed stationery which is also available at most office supply stores.

Not really hyped up on using up all your printer's ink on your wedding invitations? Take them to a specialized copy shop or office supply store. They can usually copy onto whatever paper you want (heavy card stock, pre-printed, etc.) and in color if you choose.

You could also print out simple text of your invitation then use rubber stamps or embossing powder to decorate them. Keep in mind, though, the number of invitations you'll need to embellish. If you're looking at a few hundred, you could be up nights just decorating them!

The traditional practice for wedding invitations is to put the invitation inside an envelope and then place that envelope inside another envelope. Why bother? One envelope is plenty and you'll only need one stamp to mail if you use one.

If you're doing your own invitations, check with some small local print shops for leftover envelopes they might have. You can buy these a hugely discounted price. Don't get freaked out if you have several different sizes or styles. How many people are going to ask each other at your wedding what size envelope their invitation came in?

If you need to have RSVP's, consider putting it on a small postal size card. That way you eliminate an envelope and it adds to the convenience for your guests. All they have to do is fill it out and drop it in the mailbox. Of course, you'll have to provide the stamp for this card.

Consider also printing reception information directly on the invitation itself. For an RSVP, provide a phone number and/or e-mail address for guests to respond to. Not only will this save you on postage, you'll have all the information right there for your guests to refer to before the big day instead of them having to save a separate reception card.

You can use labels to print out addresses on your computer. We would suggest getting the clear labels as it just looks better. The most prominent label maker is Avery. Their website offers free templates to print out your labels, so you may want to check that out before struggling with a software program.

If you don't like the impersonal nature of address labels, address the envelopes by hand. You can get information about calligraphy online or just use your best handwriting!

Some brides don't want the hassle of do-it-yourself invitations. We happened to have a friend who sold wedding invitations as a side business at an incredible cheap rate and she offered up a discounted rate as a wedding gift. We ended up with 300 invitations for just $60. Not everyone can be that lucky, however. Check out places online for the most savings.

Finally, when it comes to wedding invitations, one of your largest expenses is going to be the postage. You really have no control over that unless you're the Postmaster General and even then, I doubt it! You may want to hand deliver some invitations to save on postage. I know I would prefer to have the bride or groom personally hand me their invitation. It tells me I'm special to them and I know it's saving them the cost of a stamp!

So what's next? The bride, of course! Finding the perfect gown can be a long and tedious procedure. Read on for tips to save money while finding the most beautiful dress for you to say "I Do" in!

WHAT TO WEAR, WHAT TO WEAR?

Cinderella's princess gown was tailored by mice. In fairytales, that's an easy solution! In real life, it's much more daunting! Finding the perfect gown is very important to every bride to be. Most girls want to feel like a princess as they walk down the aisle to their prince charming! You can look like a princess without spending a whole month's rent on your dress!

Do you really need a hand-made wedding dress with beads and diamantes? This is where the big cost is and there are several options in cutting the cost.

First and foremost, consider wearing your mother or grandmother's wedding gown – assuming they still have them. Can you imagine the pride on their faces as they watch you stroll down the aisle toward your future husband wearing the very gown they wore doing the same thing?

Think that gown is a bit out of date? If you don't like the style, consider hiring a seamstress to update the cut a bit. You can often find a seamstress or tailor for around $100 – well less than the cost of a new, off the rack wedding gown!

Why not opt for a second-hand wedding dress? It's probably only been worn once anyway and you can get a once expensive dress for half the price. Check out consignment shops or thrift stores to see what they have to offer. Better yet, check out ebay.com. Again, if you can get a great deal on a gown and only need some alterations, a seamstress will be only a fraction of the cost to buy the gown outright.

Consider buying an evening gown/cocktail dress from a department store. Look around prom season. These days, many prom dresses can look like wedding gowns. A lot of specialty shops will run specials prior to prom hoping to cull their inventory. You can come across a great deal on a beautiful dress and look like a prom queen in the process!

For my second marriage, this is what I did. It wasn't prom season, but homecoming season. I found the most gorgeous dress off the rack that fit me like a dream. They wanted to get rid of it and I managed to talk the owner into discounting it 40%!

You may want to look around for closing out sales or liquidation sales at bridal shops in your area. One word of caution: don't drive the equivalent of halfway across the country just to find a gown. With my first wedding, they were having a going out of business sale at the local bridal shop. I found a stunning gown that retailed for $800 for a mere $100 just because it was two days before they closed their doors!

Another option is to rent your wedding gown. When my brother got married, his wife rented her gown. It was a stunning number that retailed for over $3,500. She rented it for $75. Sure, she couldn't keep it, but considering that my first wedding gown is still in the vacuum sealed box untouched for over 20 years, who really cares? I doubt my daughter will want to wear it, although I will certainly steer her toward this option – with a seamstress on stand-by, of course!

Consider shopping online at a discount wedding store or even e-bay. You won't get the pampering you do at a bridal shop, but you can save up to 40% by going this route! You can have the dress altered locally if it doesn't fit just right.

Finally, you can realize incredible savings on your dream gown by picking one out and asking a local seamstress to copy the design. This probably won't be the most cost-cutting measure, but you can have a designer gown for about half the cost you would pay directly from the designer. If you find a good seamstress, they should be able to copy the design for a significant savings.

What would be even better than that? If you or someone you know sews! Pick out a pattern at the local discount store, buy the fabric and notions, and make the dress your own, for a fraction of the cost!

What about the veil? Many brides these days eschew the traditional veil over the face in favor of a more contemporary design. That's fine and even beautiful. It's all a matter of preference! But don't fall for the inflated prices of a handmade veil at the local bridal shop.

I splurged on my first wedding for a to-die-for long beaded veil with a Juliet cap that cost more than my dress. It was a gift from my grandmother, so I didn't feel guilty. It was the ultimate headpiece for my dream wedding and I love putting it on for kicks to this day!

For my second wedding, I fell in love with a flowing tiara veil on display. The price tag, however, brought me back to reality. Imagine my surprise when my mother found a similar tiara at Claire's for $1.99 and bought the tulle for the veil at just $.99 a yard! She added satin ribbon to match the satin ribbon on my gown, and a headpiece that would have cost me over $200 adorned my head for a mere $10!

Want to know how to make your own wedding veil?

It's much easier than you think! Follow the directions below and you can have a headpiece that's amazing!

- o Start with a base. Many stores such as Claire's have cheap tiaras that can serve as your base. If you're not quite into a tiara, just have on hand some craft wire and some plastic combs to hold the veil in place.

- o Have a glue gun on hand. Get some tulle and attach it to whatever base you have. If it's a tiara, just glue directly to the headpiece. If it's combs, you'll need to create a "halo" to attach the tulle to. Add the combs so you can put it in your hair. Most tiaras come with built in combs.

- o Simply glue the tulle to your base and add any embellishments you want – flowers, baby's breath, etc. Add accents like ribbons and bows for a special look.

Also consider having simple flowers or baby's breath in your wedding coiffure. It's a beautifully simple touch to a beautiful day that will make you look like a goddess in the process!

One note here about hair and makeup. You could splurge and have a beauty shop do you and your bridal party's hair, but that's an extra expense that is really un- needed. Once again, call on family or friends to help.

Do you know someone whose hair is always stunning? See if she'll help you out. Maybe you have a distant cousin who is a hairdresser. See if she'll donate her services as a wedding gift.

When it comes to make-up, the best look is your natural look. Most people want to see the bride dressed up in her finery but looking like the same gal they know. No need to cake on foundation if you normally don't wear it. Go for some light eye shadow, mascara, a little blush and a pale lip color. You know how to do your own makeup – do it on your wedding day too.

Now that you're outfitted, what will your groom wear?

WHAT TO WEAR - FOR HIM

The traditional choice for the groom is a tuxedo.

Where I come from, buying a tuxedo is virtually unheard of. Renting is probably the way to go to realize the ultimate savings on the groom's attire. If you were to buy a tuxedo, the average cost would be somewhere between $300 and $500. This is not exactly the way to go when trying to save money on a wedding!

If you do want to buy your tux, check in thrift stores, consignment shops, and online to find discounted tuxes.

Buying off the rack will run you a lot more money.

Renting a tux will run anywhere from $50 to $100 typically. That rental will include everything your groom will need to look like Prince Charming. This means cuff links, shoes, vest, and tie.

Many places offer the grooms tux rental free when the wedding party rents from the same store. Be sure to ask about a perk like this.

If your groom wants to own his own tuxedo, we suggest a local thrift store or consignment shop. You may also want to consider a discount wedding store or even online at e-bay again.

Yet another great consideration when outfitting the guys in your wedding party is to have them wear nice suits or even casual slacks and a nice shirt. Not every wedding party has to be ultra formal; it's all up to you!

Now that you and your groom are outfitted, let's talk about those loved ones who will be standing up with you. What they wear can be just as important as what you wear!

WHAT TO WEAR - PART 2

The general rule of thumb for guys is that they will mimic what the groom is wearing. If the groom wears a tuxedo, they will wear similar tuxedos as well. If the groom is outfitted in a suit, they will wear similar suits. Remember our previous tip about renting tuxedos. Usually a rental shop will give the groom his tux rental for free if the groomsmen rent their tuxedos at the same shop. This can result in huge savings for everyone concerned!

As far as the bridesmaids are concerned, there are several more options to consider. First and foremost, the style of dress you want them to wear. Traditionally, bridesmaids are expected to pay for their own wedding attire. Because of this, you, as the bride, should use good manners when deciding on what your attendants will wear. Please remember that not all bodies are built alike and not all dress styles look good on all types of people.

In my second wedding, my attendants included my 14 year old daughter (size 0), my baby sister (size 4), and my best friend who would be 8 months pregnant on wedding day (normally size 7, but at the time of the wedding, size who knows!) My sister found 3 dresses exactly the same on clearance at a department store in the exact sizes we needed. Two of them were little bitty for her and my daughter, the third one was bigger for my friend but which we altered to fit her "condition". Total cost for all 3 dresses - $50!

Shop around are the key words here! See what you can find with the parameters you have in mind! And please remember that pink chiffon rarely works well at other places besides a wedding reception! If at all possible, pick a style that will enable the bridesmaid to wear the dress at other places and other times. This will make them less reluctant to plunk down big bucks for a dress they'll wear once and have it hang in their closet until their next rummage sale!

If you know someone who sews, pick out a pattern and fabric at your local discount store and stitch up a masterpiece.

Just as our tips for finding a wedding gown, check out the bridal shops and see what you can find off their racks. Don't be afraid to ask for a discounted price. Many times, they will grant your request just to clear their inventory!

Now that we're outfitted, what comes next? Let's look at the wedding flowers!

A ROSE IS A ROSE

Cheap doesn't mean that your wedding flowers can't be beautiful. All flowers are lovely no matter what they cost.

They can cost you a bundle, but there are many ways to save yourself a bundle as well.

The first decision to make is whether or not you want silk or real flowers. We recommend silk flowers because of the ease. However, real flowers can be a beautiful addition to your wedding. Keep in mind that real flowers need to be nurtured even up to the moment you say "I Do". If you have someone who can monitor the freshness of your real flowers, by all means, have them! If you want to save yourself and your loved ones a little stress, choose silk!

If you do choose fresh flowers, we recommend commissioning the services of a professional florist.

Working with real flowers is an art that probably shouldn't be taken on by a novice. If you do commission a florist, avoid using the "W" word (wedding) as they will most often charge you much more for wedding flowers as opposed to a few bouquets for a random event. Keep in mind that a professional florist will not save you any money. They come at a premium price, so be prepared.

Consider ordering fresh flowers from an online wholesaler. You can get some of the best prices around. However, as we mentioned, unlike at a florist, you will be responsible for all of the prep work of cleaning and trimming them, and keeping them alive until the wedding.

If you're going for a simple look, you might want to contact a local farmer. Where I live, there is an iris farm who will sell you bulk irises at a discounted rate. Find your local farmer's market and pick up some freshly cut flowers for a simple bouquet. Consider also picking flowers from your own garden.

Remember that flowers are simply garnishes. There's no need to go overboard with nosegays or hand-held masterpieces for the ceremony. The real stars of the show are you, your intended, and your wedding party. The flowers simply add to the overall package.

Consider calling a local community college for your flowers. Many local colleges offer courses in flower arranging.

For a small fee, they may be quite accommodating in allowing their students to "practice" for your wedding at a huge discounted price – often for the cost of the flowers alone. Just be prepared for what you get. It might be beautiful, it might be mediocre. As stated before, don't place too much emphasis on the flowers – they are simply garnishes.

Of course, making your own flowers is probably the most frugal choice. But where do you start? Read on!

MAKING YOUR OWN CEREMONY FLOWERS

There are plenty of wholesale stores who will sell silk flowers at a greatly discounted price. Working with silk flowers is easy and can be done by almost anyone. My mother put together all the bouquets, boutonnières, and corsages for both my weddings. She had no professional training. She simply had a bunch of flowers and some florist tape. They were utterly beautiful!

Some basic equipment you'll need are floral wire, floral tape, wire cutters, flowers, greenery, and decorative accents like baby's breath or smaller flowers. These instructions are mainly for silk flowers, but can be used with real flowers as well. Silk flowers can be manipulated much easier than real ones, so keep that in mind!

Tips for creating your own flowers are abundant. A beautifully simple idea for a gorgeous bridal bouquet is to take several white roses, bunch them together into a bouquet, wrap the bottom with floral tape tightly, and wrap satin ribbon around the stems. Attach long pieces of satin ribbon to flow down as you hold the bouquet and it'll be stunning!

You can use this technique with either silk or fresh flowers, and it doesn't have to be all roses. For a unique look, try out different flowers in your wedding colors. You can also buy plastic nosegay holders at many discount stores that make preparing bouquets super easy!

Don't worry if you can see the tape or wire. You can always disguise it with ribbon or filler.

For your bridesmaids, you can have them carry the traditional nosegay. Assemble it in the same way outlined above for the bridal bouquet. A very elegant look is to have each attendant carry a single flower or a few flowers put together with greenery and ribbon that they carry cradled in their arms. These are super easy to put together. Just take a few flowers, greenery, and accents, gather the stems together, wrap with floral tape and add ribbon.

For the boutonnières, simple is best, especially since they will be worn by the men in your wedding party. Most guys don't want garish flowers adorning their bodies – it's just a guy thing!

To put together a boutonniere, take a single flower, add a few green leaves, and maybe a sprig of baby's breath.

Wrap the stem in floral tape tightly and voila! Your bout! You can, if you wish, add a little bit of ribbon, but don't go too overboard – remember the "guy thing"!

To make corsages, use an odd number of flowers – 3 or 5 is recommended. Make it just like you would the bout, gather the stems, and add greenery and filler. You'll want the corsage to be in a round shape, or a long row. Once you have gathered all the flowers together, wrap tightly with floral tape and adjust the stems for comfort. Be sure to add some pretty ribbon for accents.

Many people just aren't sure how to pin on a corsage, so here's a most helpful tip for anyone! The corsage should bend slightly over the collar bone, so don't pin too far down. The wearer should be able to tip her head slightly to smell the flowers.

Stick the pin into the fabric at the bottom left corner of the stem. Weave the pin back out from under the fabric.

Push it through about 1 inch, laying it at an angle over the top of the stem. Stick the tip of the pin back into the fabric on the other side of the stem. Insure that the stem is tightly in place with the length of the pin pushing it down.

Weave the pin back out of the fabric once more. Be sure that the very tip of the pin does not stick out, nor does it poke under the fabric and touch the skin.

Don't forget the pins! Go for the straight pin with a pretty pearl head on it. They can be found at most craft store quite inexpensively. Have plenty on hand – just in case!

The flower girl basket is probably the easiest of all wedding ceremony flowers. Just take a small basket – preferably white – and decorate it with ribbon and some small flowers. Many local florists will sell you rose petals for the flower girl to strew down the aisle quite cheaply. If they have some roses they aren't able to sell that are going bad, they will usually part with the petals at a low price.

Just as important could be the ring bearer pillow. Want to know how to make your own? Read on!

The ring pillow from a wedding can become a treasured keepsake of a very special day and a family heirloom as well. Use high-quality materials for the pillow and be creative. Experiment with different patterns, materials and textures before you decide on a final design.

- Choose two pieces of fabric that each measure between 8 and 10 inches square. Use white or off-white satin, silk or brocade. If possible, use the same fabric and lace that is used for the wedding dress.

- Choose lace and ribbon to decorate the pillow if desired. The amounts required will depend on how the materials are used. About 2 to 3 yards each of ribbon and lace will be adequate

- Use two or three pieces of polyester batting as stuffing for the pillow. Each piece should be equal to the dimensions of the fabric squares in step 1.

- Use a fabric cutting board, ruler and fabric marking pen to mark and measure out two equal squares of fabric. Make all markings on the wrong side of the fabric. Test the pen on a scrap of the pillow fabric to make sure that the marks will fade.

- Do any embroidery or needlework before continuing to the next step. Add any other decoration to the face of the fabric as well. Embellishments such as small ribbons, charms and delicate lace can be tacked or sewn on to the fabric by hand.

❑ Add a lace ruffle to the pillow by pinning the straight edge of the ruffle to the right side of the fabric square that will form the pillow top. Pin so that the edges line up evenly and the right sides (if there is a right side to the ruffle) are together.

❑ Pin the ruffle very loosely onto the fabric or gather the ruffle slightly as you pin in order to create a fuller ruffle.

❑ Pin the fabric pieces with the right sides together. Edges should match up evenly. Pins should be placed about 1/2 inch apart and should be at right angles to the fabric edges. Make sure that the pinned edge of the ruffle is caught securely between the two fabric layers.

❑ Use a sewing machine to stitch three sides of the pillow, 1/2 inch from the fabric edges. Turn the pillow right side out and stuff the batting layers inside. If you would like a fuller pillow, insert additional batting.

❑ Fold the edges of the unsewn seam into the pillow 1/2 inch, and stitch closed by hand. Use a slipstitch done by hand or carefully topstitch the edges with your machine.

❑ Add a 10- or 12-inch length of 1/4-inch satin or silk ribbon to the top of the pillow. Stitch the ribbon by hand to the pillow at the ribbon's center point. Add a silk or satin bow made from the same ribbon to cover the stitching. Use the two ribbon strands to loosely tie the wedding rings to the pillows.

DECORATIVE FLOWERS FOR THE CEREMONY

As far as flowers and plants as decorations are concerned, this can be a great enhancement to your ceremony. Many churches already have floral adornments on their altars. If you get married around the time of a church celebration, you may be able to buy a few flowers and take advantage of those that are already there.

For example, around Easter, lilies are the flower of choice in most churches. Many people will buy Easter lilies in remembrance of their loved ones. Offer to buy a couple of Easter lilies to add to the existing ones, and you have a beautiful decoration on the altar.

The same applies around Christmas. Poinsettias are the flower of choice at this time of year. Offer up a few poinsettia plants to add to those already there and you'll have some beautiful altar decorations.

Large arrangements on an altar will only be seen from far away. Use inexpensive flowers such as carnations, or large filling flowers such as snowball mums.

If you are getting married in a church, almost all have some type of floral/tree decorations that they have all the time. All you need to do in this situation is to add a few personal touches and you'll have a beautiful backdrop for your ceremony. This is what we did for my second marriage. We took the artificial fichus trees and arranged them around our other flowers to make for a beautiful altar.

If you are getting married outside, take advantage of nature. Cultivate what Mother Nature has to offer. When my cousin got married, he did so at a local park overlooking a lake. The flowers were in full bloom and it was beautiful. His wife later told me that she had been out at that park every day for two weeks just to make sure that the flowers would be gorgeous -- and they were!

Talk to your venues and see if any other brides have booked for the same day. If the two of you can coordinate flowers and split the cost, you'll save a lot of money. I would imagine both of you wouldn't turn your nose up at saving a ton of money on church decorations and flowers!

Some party rental places will rent large potted plants such as tropical palms or fichus. They visually fill a lot of space, and will help frame your ceremony site or warm up your reception. Best of all, renting a potted plant is far cheaper than buying large flower arrangements. Also, you may consider purchasing these large plants and using them in your home afterwards to get more use out of them.

Almost everyone I knew owned an artificial fichus tree, so I made several phone calls and asked if we could borrow them for our big day. Everyone was more than happy to offer up their trees and we used them to decorate the reception hall. More on that later!

Don't try to move your ceremony flowers to the reception hall. Many churches require you leave them anyway, but moving large arrangements can be tedious and simply not worth the time or effort. The last thing you want is to have your reception held up waiting for flowers!

Decorating the place where you will take your vows is just as important as how you decorate your reception. Let's look at how to make your ceremony picture perfect!

DECORATING THE CEREMONY

We've covered the floral decorations for a church wedding, but what else do you need to decorate the

sanctuary. Because you're on a budget, remember that less is more. Most wedding ceremonies are short and sweet, so why spend a majority of your money decorating a place where people are most likely only going to be for a half hour or so?

If you want pew bows, they can be made quite inexpensively, but don't decorate each pew. Decorate every other one for the first 10 rows or so. Ribbon for bows can get quite expensive, so doing every other pew is the frugal thing to do.

MAKING YOUR OWN PEW BOWS

Speaking from experience, initial bow making can be extremely frustrating. Give yourself plenty of time and practice when you start this craft. While it may take a few tries to finally master it, once you do, you'll start cranking out the bows fairly quickly. Below are instructions for two different types of bows that can be layered for a more elaborate effect:

You will need approximately 4.5 feet of 1" wired ribbon; approximately 4.5 feet of 6" tulle (more or less depending on how long you want the tails); craft wire, wire cutter, scissors.

The Tulle Base:

1. Lay the ribbon horizontally. Find the middle of your strip of tulle and pinch together with your left hand.
2. With your right hand, pinch the tulle on the right side about 8" away from the middle.

3. Bring the second pinched spot to the center, moving underneath. This should form half of a bow. Pinch together the middle with your right hand.

4. Repeat the same thing with the left side, only this time instead of bringing the tulle underneath to form the bow, bring it over the top.

5. You should now have a simple bow. Secure the middle by twisting craft wire around it. If you'd like to stop here, hot glue a silk flower in the middle to finish this simple project. However, if you want your bow more ornate, follow the next set of instructions to add a second layer.

The Second Ribbon Layer:

1. Lay the wired ribbon vertically on a table or flat surface, moving away from you. Take the end closest to you, bring it up and then tuck it in to form a small loop. Pinch the loop in place. This will be the middle of the ribbon.

2. Just after where you are now pinching, twist the longer end of the ribbon 180 degrees. Keep the twist tight and "hide" it underneath the middle loop. Grab the long

piece of ribbon about 6" away from the middle. Then form a loop by bringing the ribbon underneath and back to the center. Pinch together.

3. Twist the long piece of ribbon again just after the center pinch. Make an equal sized loop on the other side using the same technique.

4. Continue making equal-sized loops that rest directly underneath each other by using the same technique. Stop when you have three on each side.

5. Secure the middle with craft wire and leave some extra wire in order to attach it to the tulle base.

6. Cut off any tail you might have left over from the ribbon.

7. Spread out the loops to create the look you desire.

Attaching:

With the extra wire from the second layer, attach the ribbon bow to the middle of the tulle base. Consider adding long wire hooks or extra ribbon to the back for easy attachment to the pews.

You may want to consider using simple floral swags at the end of each pew as well. These can be found inexpensively and made even more inexpensively!

Many churches have single candle holders that you can use or rent for a nominal fee. If you are a member of the church, ask! The clergy has had exposure to many weddings. He or she might have some terrific, low-cost ideas you may not have thought about!

What we did for my second wedding was an idea I had never seen before. My mother went to a discount store and found battery operated candles – the kind people put in their windows around Christmas time – on clearance. They can also be found at craft stores or craft warehouses pretty cheaply.

Mom attached a Velcro strip to the bottom of each candle and got permission from the church to attach a strip to the end of each pew. We bought a huge pack of batteries and attached one to the end of each pew. My 8 year old cousin was responsible for twisting the base of each candle to turn them on right before the ceremony – a job she was quite proud of – and we had a gorgeously lit sanctuary!

If you're planning an outdoor wedding, the scenery will be your most dramatic decoration. Most couples opt for the traditional gazebo or arch when getting married outdoors.

I've seen these on sale at a local wholesaler before at a mere $19.99! You can also rent the archway from a party rental place. Decorate it with flowers, Christmas lights, or greenery to make it beautiful.

Seating at an outdoor wedding usually consists of folding chairs. These can usually be found at a benevolent association like The American Legion – excellent place to find seating especially if you're having your reception there - churches, or community centers. Even if you have to pay a few dollars to rent them, it will be worth it!

Decorate the ends of the chairs with greenery and flowers to match your wedding bouquets along with strategically placed ribbon. To set off the "important guest" area (parents, grandparents, etc.) cover the backs of the chairs with simple white pillowcases.

All weddings are made much more special with an added touch contributed by music before, during, and after the ceremony.

MUSIC AT YOUR CEREMONY

Music for your wedding ceremony could consist of live or recorded performances. For pre-wedding music, make a CD of songs that are meaningful to you as a couple. You can also use this CD for the processional and recessional marches.

Do you know someone who plays the piano or guitar?

Ask them to play for you at your ceremony. Nothing sounds as poignant as an acoustic guitar playing a beautiful ballad! Call your local high school or college for musicians.

Recruit someone you know to sing during the ceremony. If you don't know anyone who sings, find a place where they're having karaoke and pick the singer you like best. Offer them a small fee to sing at your wedding and – VOILA! – You have a vocalist to make your day special!

You want to be sure to have plenty of photos to remember your special day. Unfortunately, a professional photographer can be a real budget buster! Read on for tips on how to save with wedding photography.

SMILE PRETTY

Pictures are priceless, and you want to be sure you have plenty of good pictures of your special day.

Unfortunately, if you're on budget, professional photographers can eat up most of your money. While they are definitely worth the price, they're not always feasible for people who need to save some money.

So how can you get beautiful photos of your wedding day without breaking the bank? Let me tell you what we did.

With my first wedding, we were definitely on a budget and in no position to pay the $900 a professional photographer was asking – and that was in 1985! My mother worked for a local newspaper and asked the head photographer there if he would be willing to take wedding photos for us.

We paid for the film and developing, he took the pictures, and he got to eat and party at our reception. The pictures were beautiful and we made our own albums at a fraction of the cost.

Today, the local Wal-Mart or photo processing studio will provide you with enlargements quite cheaply.

For my second wedding, we called on family. You will see this same theme throughout this book when it came to my second marriage. My husband and I had lived together for 8 years and were not really in need of a formal china service or a third toaster – although we did need towels and sheets! Most of my family was happy to offer up their services in place of a wedding gift.

My cousin is an amateur photography buff. She was more than happy to offer up her services to us. Once again, we bought the film and paid for the developing while she took the pictures and enjoyed the reception. This was no small feat as just two months prior to my wedding, she found out she was two months pregnant with triplets and was unsure she could even make the ceremony as it was a high-risk pregnancy.

Luckily, she was there and we got some beautiful pictures. Two months after that, I had two amazing boy cousins and a precious little girl cousin join my family, so even though she offered up her services as our wedding photographer as a wedding present, we still provided her with a gift certificate to a local spa after the babies came as a special little extra for her effort and commitment to us!

So how can you find similar services? We recommend you start with a community college. They often offer photography classes, and the students are eager to practice their craft for a nominal fee or even just the experience.

Talk to the instructor, however, to be sure you're getting the cream of the crop – the top in the class. You don't want to take a chance and get the beginner for your big day.

Ask friends and family to see if anyone likes to experiment with photography as a hobby. Film can be bought in bulk at warehouse stores, so if you have them take a multitude of pictures, you'll probably get more than several that are exactly what you wanted.

Don't be afraid to call the local newspaper and ask to speak with the staff photographer. You don't have to know anyone at the paper to offer up the chance for them to make some extra money. Many will perform the service for a small fee as long as you buy the film – some may even offer their services for the experience.

At the reception, place disposable cameras on each table for guests to take pictures at your reception. A word of caution here: place a note on the table that asks the adults to please monitor the use of these cameras. I have been to many a reception where children have gotten hold of these cameras and the bride was left with many, many pictures of people's feet and – um – hind ends!

Disposable cameras can be found – again – at bulk warehouse stores or even online. Shop around for the best price and use them sparingly. If you don't want to put the cameras on the table, another idea is to place the cameras in a basket at the door as guests enter the reception. The ones who really care about taking pictures will take the cameras. Have your guest book attendant monitor who takes them or even have the attendant hand them out to adults only.

When it comes to chic, elegant wedding pictures, nothing beats the look of Black and White photos. Black and White photos can be combined with all of the money saving ideas above. After the wedding, the photos can be blown up and dry mounted for a long-lasting keepsake. Black and white film can be much cheaper than color film as well.

As far as video is concerned, consider what a video will mean to you. Sure, a video of your wedding is a pretty nice thing to have, but let's face it, who really watches this video? Your family may watch it once after the wedding is over, and you and your future spouse may bring it out on your anniversary every year, but other than that the most public viewing of your wedding video will probably be at your 50th anniversary party

(and by then you will have had to pay a couple hundred dollars to have your video converted to the latest format. ex. DVD)

I think a great way to save a thousand bucks is to ask yourself and family before your wedding, "Who owns a video camera that I know?" "Who do I know who has a hobby of videotaping?" Maybe you know one person who owns a video camera but hates to tape, and another person who has the patience and artistic ability to video, but doesn't own a camera. Voila! You have your own videographer, if both parties are willing to play their part (and I think you will find that almost everyone is willing to help in whatever small way they can to help make your wedding a success).

Of course, it would probably be a good idea to lay down some rules for your videographer since they are using someone else's camera (such as, keep the camera with you at all times and don't let anyone else use the camera, etc.)

Video was virtually unheard of at my first wedding, but at my second wedding, my step-dad wanted a behind-the- scenes role, so he volunteered to man the video camera.

When we got to the reception, he set up the camera on a tripod and caught some very personal moments when the time dictated.

I can honestly say that after 5 years of marriage, I have only watched my wedding video twice. I'm glad I have it, but if I would have had to pay a large amount of money to have it professionally done, I would be a bit sick.

If you do have a friend or family member do your wedding video, there are many studios around who can cut and splice parts of the video together and add background music later if you want a precious keepsake. You can do this later, however, when you can afford it and not have to figure it into your wedding budget.

Once the wedding has finished, it's time to move to the reception. Let's consider different way to decorate your reception location.

DECORATING THE RECEPTION HALL

Your wedding reception is where your guests will spend the most time. As we've said before, you should count on spending at least 40 percent of your budget on the reception. This includes the food, decorations, drinks, music, etc. But a beautiful reception doesn't have to break the bank. Once again, count on your friends and family to help out. I can't tell you how many halls I've decorated just because someone called. If you're a benevolent soul like I am, call in your favors when your big day comes!

Let's first talk about the flowers and table decorations.

If you're having your reception in a hall like the Legion or the moose, be prepared to deal with the décor that is already there. We had my second reception at the legion and there was a multitude of war memorabilia everywhere. Since war and war heroes wasn't the focus of my wedding, we found ourselves daunted by the various wall hangings that existed.

What we decided to do was create a lighted wonderland. We called upon everyone we could think of to lend us their white Christmas lights. We married at the end of January, so the Christmas décor was freshly put away or still stowed in the garage waiting for permanent stashing until the next season. We ended up with about 200 strands of lights.

We strung them everywhere – from the ceiling, woven throughout the fichus trees, even framing the confederate soldier uniform. When the lights went out, no one knew that we were in a memorialized hall to our military veterans.

We brought the battery operated candles from the church and put them on all the tables. My uncle had some butcher paper that we spread over all the tables for tablecloths and every other one had floating candles in glass vases that we found wholesale at a craft store.

We sprinkled blue glitter on the tables for a little glitz. If you decide to do this, take my advice, use it sparsely and keep it mostly toward the center of the table! Glitter can be a huge mess if it's strewn about too randomly! It looks great, but some guests won't be crazy about getting glitter on their "good" clothes!

So what about other decorative ideas at the reception? Use the bridesmaid's bouquets to decorate the tables, the head table, or the cake table. You don't have to have expensive floral

59

arrangements everywhere to make a beautiful reception hall. There are many, many alternatives and most can be put together with supplies from the dollar store. The following suggestions utilize supplies that I found at the dollar store and make for gorgeous table decorations.

Centerpiece suggestion #1:

Buy some glass cereal bowls and place colored glass marbles in the bottom. Add water half way up and put a floating candle in each. Instead of floating candles, just add a regular votive in the middle of the marbles. When the reception is over, the bride and groom will have a matching set of bowls!

Centerpiece suggestion #2:

Get some small terracotta pots and some florists foam. Pick out some silk flowers in your wedding colors along with some greenery. Stick the flowers in the foam bunched tightly together and arrange to your heart's delight!

Centerpiece suggestion #3:

Take a silk rose and separate the bud from the stem.

Disassemble the bud into individual petals. With a clear votive holder and a glue gun, you will glue the petals onto the holder. Start at the top with the smaller rose petals. Place one petal next to another, with the sides touching slightly.

Once your first row is completed, you can start on the next. Make sure to cover any bare areas at the bottom of the first row, and work your way down the holder until the rose petals cover the entire surface. Take the leaf from the flower and attach to the bottom of the holder. This will give the illusion of a lighted rose once a candle is placed inside and lit!

Centerpiece suggestion #4:

Find picture frames of varying sizes. Gather together your favorite pictures of the bride and groom. Put the pictures in the frames and arrange on the tables surrounding them by clear glass marbles and some greenery.

Centerpiece suggestion #5:

Get some small baskets and decorate with ribbon.

Print out some index cards that say "Advice For The Newlyweds" and lay them on the table with pens and/or pencils. Encourage guests to write something on the cards and place them in the baskets. Surround the baskets with flowers, greenery or pebbles. This can be a great ice-breaker for people who don't know each other. Be prepared, too, for the jokesters in the crowd who may offer up some ridiculous and sometimes bawdy advice.

Centerpiece suggestion #6:

Take small grapevine wreaths and decorate with tulle and ribbon. Place a bottle of champagne in the center or a bottle of wine from a local winery. For extra fun, attach a balloon to the bottle.

Centerpiece suggestion #7:

Take two plastic champagne glasses and hot glue them together so that they cross when laying down. Hot glue four clear glass marbles inside each glass and tie a helium balloon to each. It will look like there are bubbles flowing out of your glasses as they lay on the table!

We had balloons at both of my wedding receptions.

Not only are they festive and fun, they can help keep bored children entertained. Most dollar stores have helium balloons they will fill with purchase. However, you may want to look into a portable helium tank and do it yourself. I found one at Wal-Mart for $19.99 with balloons at $.99 a bag. The tank filled up about 40 balloons so that's one way to save a little money on your balloons.

Want some wacky and unique centerpiece ideas? We found a couple online for the inventive and fun couples!

Buy glass fish bowls at the dollar store and fill them with – fish! You can find goldfish pretty inexpensively either at Wal-Mart or a local pet store. If you have the money, try to find beta fish in your wedding colors! One word of caution if using live fish: be sure to give their water lots of surface area to provide enough oxygen. The last thing you want is a bunch of dead fish decorating your tables. Let the children in attendance take the fish home – with the permission of their parents, of course.

One couple wanted to be whimsical at their reception, so they collected up all the board games they loved as children – Ants in the Pants, Monopoly, Sorry, etc. These were arranged on the tables with decorative accents surrounding them. This can be great for the children in attendance, but don't be surprised if the adults play with them too.

Another bride wanted to reflect the personalities of her and her groom. They were "country people", she says and liked a cold beer on occasion. She took longneck beer bottles and steamed the labels off of them. She created their own beer labels on her computer and glued them on with a hot glue gun. She splatter painted them before attaching the labels and tied each with a piece of twine.

Truly unique, we think!

We like the idea of taking a pint sized Mason jar and wrapping it with tissue paper tying a ribbon around the neck to secure it. Place flowers in the jar, potpourri or whatever you think fits you as a couple.

If you're getting married around a holiday, you can come across some fun decorations that celebrate that holiday. At Christmas, spray paint pine cones silver and gold and surround them with pine sprigs. Having an Easter wedding? Use plastic Easter eggs and that annoying plastic grass you put in the Easter baskets.

If you're having an outdoor reception, decorate around that. Use lots of live flowers and greenery to reflect the beauty of Mother Nature surrounding you. If it's windy, avoid using candles and be sure any balloons are secured so they don't blow away!

Now that you've got the place decorated, you may want to consider using favors as additional decorations.

WEDDING FAVORS

Some brides don't like the idea of giving gifts to her guests, but we think it's a nice gesture as a thank you for attending your special day. These favors can be elegant, fun, or practical. We prefer the practical. Here are some great suggestions for fun and unique wedding favors.

- Divinity fudge makes delicious cheap wedding favors. Wrapped up in white tulle and tied with a white ribbon it would be beautiful. Add a tag; you make yourself, with a little message like "Love is divine". Cut out the tag with scallop scissors and punch a hole for the ribbon. One warning, divinity doesn't come out well in high humidity.

- Regular candles are nice too for cheap wedding favors. Wrap in tulle and tie with ribbon. Stick a small flower in the ribbon.

- Tree seedlings, such as citrus or any kind of tree, are something everybody would love. They will always remember your wedding with this unique wedding favor idea. Wrap the plastic pot to disguise.

- Flower seedlings or seed packets are a nice wedding favors. Wrap in anyway that is appropriate for your wedding. Tie with ribbon, raffia or paper ribbon.

- Make wine glass markers from wire and beads. You can find instructions at the craft store. One is enough for a wedding party favor. Place in a small box and tie with ribbon.

- Sachets made from lavender. Make a small bag from lace. Sew up three sides, put the lavender in and sew up fourth side. Attach a small silk flower. Potpourris in drawstring bags made of lace or tulle are pretty. They smell nice too. You can use any kind of bag that's easy for you to make.

- Everybody loves herbs. Buy small ones and place plastic container right into a small terracotta pot. Put some moss around the top to disguise the plastic planter.

Include a pretty tag with instructions for care and attach to a ribbon tied around the pot.

- A strawberry plant is another live wedding favor idea. It can be presented in the same way as an herb. Anything of this nature that is in season is appreciated.

- Candies, such as M&Ms in your wedding colors, Kisses or Hugs, mints, a wonderful piece of chocolate or any kind that you would like, look great in a cupcake liner. They come in different sizes and colors.

- Get M and M's in your wedding colors (www.colorworks.com), place them in plastic bags and tie a ribbon on them.

- For an outdoor wedding, consider buying umbrellas for a dollar a piece at the dollar store. Wrap them in ribbons with your colors. This, of course, is for a smaller wedding only, but can be a great gift to help shield guests from inclement weather or the sun.

- Buy plain chocolate bars in bulk or get the miniature version. Print out new labels on your computer that you personalize for yourself and wrap them around the bars.

- Make your own CD using your favorite songs. Include the First Dance song, the cake-cutting song and all the traditional songs. Make CD covers with your picture on it and gave all your guests a copy of the CD. You can also make general mix CD's with all of your favorite songs on it – not just the wedding ones!

- For a Christmas wedding, give each guest a Christmas ornament. Take a plain ball type ornament and use a paint pen to personalize with your name and the date of your wedding

- Do you and your intended share a love of something unique? Are you big Nascar fans? Love to golf? Rabid about a sports team? Gear your favors around these unique characteristics that are you.

Also, unless you have your heart set on taking home your table decorations, consider giving them away to guests. A fun way to do this is to take a hint from most class reunions. Give one to the guests that traveled the farthest, the ones who have married the longest, married the shortest, etc. This helps bring people into your reception and make them feel like a bigger part of your special day!

Perhaps the largest expense of your reception is food. Let's look at some viable options for feeding you and your guests without having to mortgage your house.

YUMMY YUMMY

Food can take a huge chunk out of your wedding budget. It's often difficult to figure out what's acceptable as it is an area in which expert's (etiquette or otherwise) opinions vary widely. It can also be difficult to choose what type of food to serve at your reception... especially when you consider all of the different varieties of food available to you.

If you are having your reception at a hall that offers food service as part of the package, choose your menu wisely. While you may dream of a steak and lobster meal at your reception, this will be quite expensive and is not really viable when throwing a wedding on a budget.

There's nothing wrong with an elegantly prepared chicken breast for your wedding meal. Perhaps offer a vegetarian alternative like fish as well. Beef tends to be more expensive than poultry or fish, so be completely committed if you must have steak, you'll pay for it!

Consider having hors d'ouevres if your reception hall will be catering. Almost always, these will be cheaper than a sit down meal, and guests can enjoy them just as much.

Here are some general tips for your wedding dinner catered by your reception hall:

- It's a myth that a buffet-style meal is less expensive than a served one. In reality, buffets require more food and more labor so their cost is higher.

- If you are working with a smaller group (say 40 to 70), piggyback onto another group's menu. This allows the hotel to buy in bulk and lowers your price.

- Whenever possible, order in bulk yourself.

- Consider other main entrees besides beef and chicken. Chefs can do a lot of things with pastas and the price is usually very reasonable

- Allow the chef to try out his new, original recipes with your group. Most welcome the chance to be creative and lower the price per serving in exchange for the group's feedback. Be careful that it's not something too exotic, though. Lamb or swordfish might not appeal to everyone in your party!

- Negotiate house wine price with dinner versus a specialty wine.

- Find out how the caterer/hotel taxes food. If gratuity is part of the taxed bill, the cost will be more.

For halls that will allow you to bring in your own caterer, the key here is to shop around. Check with a local family restaurant and see if they have bulk meals they will offer for your reception. Almost all will or at the very least, will try for the money.

At my first wedding, we did this. At just $2.15 a plate for 200 people, we got fried chicken and ham, mashed potatoes, green beans, corn, rolls, butter, coffee, tea, and all the utensils including plates and napkins. All of our guests ate till they were full and we had food left over! It was very much worth the cost.

The truly frugal bride will probably want to do what we did at my second wedding, though. As I've mentioned – what is this, the hundredth time? – Family and friends pitched in a lot for us as a wedding gift.

My uncle has a business where he smokes meat for people. He smoked some pork butts that I got discounted from the local butcher. We shredded the meat and added barbeque sauce for pork sandwiches. The buns were bought at Aldi for $.29 a package.

My dad has a rather large family which provides me with 4 aunts along with 2 other ladies I consider family making 6 "aunts" in total. Each offered up a dish for my reception. One made macaroni salad, one made potato salad. We had coleslaw, a green tossed salad, green bean casserole, and baked beans. I bought huge bags of potato chips and all the utensils in bulk at Sam's Club, and we had a simple, homemade, and very tasty meal.

Along those lines, you may want to explore a potluck reception.

The Potluck Reception

Don't be shy to pursue this potluck reception idea. It is truly the traditional way to celebrate. And, it is truly the number one low budget wedding option.

Today's weddings are so commercialized. You will learn that caterers offer very limited menus to very limited budgets! Guests will likely be very pleased and welcome the idea of a potluck reception.

The potluck reception goes well with any wedding theme. If you are shy about approaching this option you can simply call it an "Old Time Traditional Wedding Celebration" The potluck dinner will suit this theme quite naturally and no-one will even question it!

You may even want to pick an "Old Time" theme for your decorating and favors. This will further incorporate the idea of an old time tradition theme. Why not try a 50's theme or a 20's theme. These are both popular old time themes.

Simply slip an added note with the invite, or on the invite, to give guests this option. For example the note might read...

Our reception will be an "Old Time Traditional Celebration" with a potluck dinner.

Please check here if you would like to bring a dish for the reception in place of a wedding gift. Call with dish suggestions please.

Have them call to get or offer suggestions on a dish so you have control over the menu. No one is obligated to participate, but I'm sure you will be surprised at how many guests will opt for this.

You and your guests will be equally surprised at the great variety and quality of the dishes provided. Guests will want to bring only their best recipes to a grand occasion such as a wedding reception!

Here are some descriptions of a few reception types in which a full meal is not served. All of these options are less expensive than a full meal (whether buffet style or sit-down) if you are willing to do most of the work yourself. All of these receptions are acceptable if you aren't holding the reception during meal-time.

Breakfast is often served around 8:00 a.m., Lunch at 12:00 p.m. and Dinner at 6:00 p.m., and these are the times in which a full meal is generally expected by guests. These times also vary depending on your area. You should hold your reception two hours before or after these times if not considering a full meal.

Cake and Punch Reception - The most common time of day that this type of reception is held is early afternoon (approximately 2:00 p.m.), but it can also occur in mid- morning (approximately 10:00 a.m.). A cake and punch reception generally consists of the wedding cake and refreshments. Refreshments can include: punch, coffee, tea, champagne, etc. You can also supplement the wedding cake with other types of cake in different flavors and textures.

Dessert Reception - This type of reception is one in which desserts are served. Desserts can include pies, cakes, doughnuts, cookies, pastries, brownies, etc. Another option, which can be combined with a normal dessert reception if you'd like, is a sundae bar.

In this type of reception, you serve bowls of ice cream (usually vanilla) and let your guests choose their topping.

Toppings can include chocolate or fudge sauce, shredded coconut, chocolate chips, crushed walnuts, whipped cream, fruit toppings, etc. Basically, the same things you'd find in any sundae bar. Summer is the most common time of year for a sundae bar. A normal dessert bar can be used year round though as there are desserts specific to season. For example, pumpkin pie and apple pie would be a great choice for fall weddings. This type of reception is also an example of an inexpensive choice if you purchase the items on your own.

Hors D'ouevres Reception - There are actually two distinct types of hors d'ouevres receptions. The first is light hors d'ouerves and consists of a lighter fare than the second which is a heavy hors d'ouerves menu.

A light menu often includes items such as: crackers, vegetable platters with dip, fruit, cheese, etc. A heavy hors d'ouerves often includes these as well as items such as: meat and cheese trays, chicken fingers, egg rolls, etc.

These types of receptions are also (casually) called "finger-food receptions" in some areas. In order to save money on this type of reception, check your local grocery store deli for prices on "meat and cheese" trays as well as "vegetable" and "cracker and cheese" platters. Their prices are often very reasonable. Another option is to buy the ingredients yourself.

Tea (or Coffee) Reception - This type of reception is a relic from a bygone era. Originally, tea receptions were meant to reflect the mood of an "afternoon tea." An authentic tea reception will include items such as petit fours, watercress sandwiches, cucumber sandwiches, scones (biscuits), etc. Be sure to cut the crusts off the sandwiches and cut in a diagonal cross (X shape) for an authentic look. If you're looking for a more modern approach...you can serve coffee with (or in place of) the tea. You can also serve: bite-size pieces of cake (such as carrot), any manner of sandwich which is easy to cut, cinnamon rolls, etc. This type of reception is relatively inexpensive (depending on the items you decide to serve) and can be relaxing for both the couple and the guests.

Salad Reception - This choice is becoming more popular and is a viable choice for vegetarians who don't want to serve a full meal. Items served can include: green (lettuce, spinach) salads, fruit salads, pasta salads, potato salads (lacto-ovo), coleslaw (lacto- ovo), etc.

A veggie bar (to supplement green salads) can be added as well and may have such choices as: chopped onions, carrots (baby or sliced), celery, broccoli, mushrooms, diced tomatoes, sliced cucumbers, etc.

A salad dressing bar can be chosen as well and may include such choices as: vinegar and oil, Italian dressing, garlic and olive oil, balsamic vinegar and lemon juice, etc. If you're a lacto-ovo vegetarian other dressing choices could include: bleu cheese, green goddess, ranch, French, etc. This type of reception is also inexpensive if you prepare most of the items yourself.

Some other general ideas for do-it-yourself food at the reception include:

- Try a pasta reception in which your guests are served plain pasta with their choice of toppings

- Have a Mexican buffet

- Provide simple lunch meats and cheeses with bread for sandwiches

- If you're a member of a church and will be having your reception there, check with the ladies auxiliary and see if they'll do the food in exchange for a donation to their organization.

- Try a local service organization: the Kiwanis, the Jaycees

- Call a community college and see if their culinary students would cook for you if you provide the food

There is some debate on whether it's a good idea to add a line on your invitation stating what type of reception is occurring. Some examples of this are: "Cake and Punch Reception to Follow Ceremony", "Light hors d'ouevres reception to follow at two o'clock" and "Dessert Reception Following Ceremony".

My personal opinion is that it makes it easier--not only for the couple...but for the guests as well. It's a clear way for the couple to inform guests that a full meal should not be expected...and guests have the option of eating a meal (if needed) prior to or after the wedding.

Another important aspect of cuisine at the wedding is the cake. You don't have to spend a fortune to have a delicious and beautiful wedding cake.

CALLING BETTY CROCKER!

Your cake is the centerpiece of the reception. It is a scrumptious dessert as well as part of a tradition- the beautiful or messy cutting-of-the-cake.

Look at lots of different ideas before you decide what you want. Visit bakeries and peruse bridal magazines. You might also find inspiration at a toy store, in china patterns or from your favorite candies.

Remember fancy cakes from the bakery are expensive, anywhere from three dollars to fifteen dollars a slice plus other charges like delivery, etc.

Simple cakes can be very elegant. We'll give you great ideas to have a marvelous confection that will long be remembered after it's eaten and smashed in the face of the bride and groom.

Consider simplicity with your cake. The actual one you have on display doesn't have to fee your entire guest list.

Try out a simple two-tiered number and then have a sheet cake in the kitchen to serve to guests.

Why not try cupcakes as an alternative to the traditional tiered cake. These can be made in a variety of flavors and arranged on a tiered rack or in a creative design on the cake table.

Of course, the best way to save the most on a wedding is to make it yourself or have a friend or relative bake it.

Consider the cost of some cake mixes and frosting, and you can see how baking your own cake can save money.

Wedding cakes don't have to be elaborate, just tasty.

When decorating, consider using fresh flowers. This will add some real class to the cake and bring in the colors of your wedding too.

The cake topper is another place where you can show your uniqueness as a couple. My second husband and I are avid golfers. My mom found some miniature (really small) plastic drivers that just happened to be white. She tied them together with ribbon and this is what adorned our cake.

Consider a matchbox car for the Nascar fans. How about one of those headliner figures in your favorite team for a sports couple? Do you both like to fish? No, don't put a fish on top of your cake, but you can put a lure or bobber up there. Please, though, buy it new – don't just grab something from your tackle box!

Many couples want to have mints and nuts to go along with the cake. This is fine, but you should buy the nuts in bulk from a warehouse store, and make the mints yourself. Homemade mints can be frozen well in advance and still taste delicious when they're thawed out.

Try this delicious recipe:

WEDDING CREAM MINTS

1 three-ounce package cream cheese softened 3 cups powdered sugar

Food coloring (in your wedding colors)

Flavoring (available at most grocery stores) – peppermint preferably

Mix cheese, flavoring, and coloring till well blended. Slowly add sugar. Knead in with fingers as mixture thickens. Roll into small balls then into granulated sugar. Press flat with a spoon. Refrigerate or freeze. If freezing, thaw in refrigerator 1-2 days prior to serving.

This makes 50-75 mints. Plan 2 mints per person.

Guests cannot have food and cake alone at your reception. Let's explore the question of beverages.

TO PARTY OR NOT TO PARTY

The question of whether or not to serve alcohol at your wedding is one that can cause dissension in the ranks of family. We'll address that in a moment.

Plan to have on hand coffee. You can borrow a large coffee dispenser from the local church, or your reception hall will probably have one on hand for you to use. Buy a large can of coffee on sale and brew it yourself.

Iced tea is always good to have as well. You can get family size tea bags at most grocery stores and brew the tea in your coffee pot. Rinse it out good first! Put the brewed tea in a large cooler dispenser, add some water and ice. If you want to add sugar, do, but many guests prefer to add their own, so we suggest leaving it unsweetened and providing sugar at the tables.

Soda can be expensive, but is a great hit with the kids! Buy 2 liter bottles and plastic cups instead of cans. Have a large cooler filled with ice as well. We recommend the smaller cups since the guests are more likely to drink it all instead of leaving some in the bottom. It's a small way to conserve on the amount used. Unless you're rabid about the taste of name-brand sodas, the store brand can often be just as good and much less expensive.

Punch is always good to have at a wedding reception. We're willing to bet you know someone who owns a punch bowl, so borrow it. Don't go overboard on the punch, though. Many people will only have a cup or two and you don't want to have leftover. It's not that great the second day!

A good basic punch recipe is to mix together a 2 liter bottle of lemon-lime soda, a can/bottle of fruit punch, andflavored sherbet. You can also use plain vanilla ice cream. Stir together until the sherbet or ice cream is melted. Add ice.

Now let's address the alcohol question. For some people, it's a no-brainer. No alcohol, no drunken relatives to spoil the day. In many families, this option is a must. I'm reminded of the reception where the bride's grandma got drunk and picked a fight with the groom's grandma. They ended up tangling on the floor and an ambulance had to be called. No bride wants that as a memory of their special day.

Where I come from, it's just not a proper wedding reception without drinks. For the frugal bride on a budget, however, alcohol can be a huge cost. There are ways you can save if you will be having cocktails at your wedding.

First, you need to check with your reception hall to see if you must purchase liquor directly from them or if you can bring it in yourself. If you have to get it from them, negotiate a price. They're usually willing to give a little knowing that you're investing your money in them for the reception.

Most people can't afford to have an open bar for the duration of the reception. Just to clarify, an open bar is one where guests can drink whatever and how much they want and the bride and groom pay the bill.

We suggest having open bar for only an hour or two.

You can calculate just how much you're able to pay for a bar bill and instruct the bartender to cut off the open bar when you've reached that point.

Some experts think it's an insult to ask guests to pay for their own drinks. We beg to differ on this point.

Drinking is optional. With the couple providing a meal, music, and socialization, asking them to pay for everyone's drunk is just not feasible for the everyday Joe.

If you do want to have an open bar, it's a good idea to limit that to beer and wine only and opting out of pricey mixed drinks that can add up quickly. Insist that bartenders use shot glasses.

This keeps drinks uniform, and if you're charged per bottle, prevents bartenders from "pouring heavy" to go through more bottles.

If you are allowed to provide your own liquor, this, of course, would be the best way to save on alcohol at your wedding. For large groups, buy beer by the keg, not the bottle. Contact a nearby winery and ask about bulk discounts. Buy liquor at warehouse stores like Sam's or Costco as well.

Don't think you have to have absolutely every type of liquor on hand. If guests want an exotic drink, they're out of luck. Buy only the basics: vodka, whiskey, rum, and possibly gin. We suggest having on hand some juices as well: orange, cranberry, and pineapple. You should also have cola and lemon-lime sodas.

We strongly suggest having a bartender on hand instead of asking your guests to make their own drinks. You might find yourself running out of liquor quite quickly that way! Perhaps enlist the services of a friend to pour drinks.

Better yet, ask several friends to take a turn for an hour at a time. Your reception hall might have someone willing to do it as well.

A rather unconventional, but sometimes feasible idea for liquor is to have guests bring their own alcohol. That way, they have what they prefer, and you don't have the expense!

Also, consider making your own wine spritzers. One couple I know rented a champagne fountain from a party rental place and put the spritzer in it instead of champagne. Mix equal parts of lemon-lime soda and wine and you have a tasty alternative to straight wine or beer.

For my first wedding, we were very limited on our budget for alcohol. We had purchased 3 kegs of beer wholesale from a family friend who owned a liquor store, but my future in-laws (at the time) wanted to have liquor available too. What did we do? Raided the liquor cabinets at home! We were able to purchase a few bottles, but when we brought together what we found in both my parents house and their house, we had a lot of alcohol available and took home what wasn't used.

Above all, make sure that any of your guests who have had too much to drink won't be driving home. You may want to have on hand the number of a taxi service or provide one yourself with teenage family members. Have someone in charge of keeping an eye on those who are inebriated and someone else to enforce the requirement that they not drink and drive. They may be angry that night, but they'll thank you in the morning – through the haze of their hangover!

The final aspect of your reception you'll need to decide on is music.

BOOGIE OOGIE OOGIE

A wedding reception is a party to celebrate the union of two special people. Most celebrations include music to express the joy everyone is feeling. What are your options when you're on a budget? Varied!

Most people like to have a disc jockey at their reception - if only because they have a large selection of music available to please the various age groups you'll have there. Disc jockeys are probably less expensive than bands, but they can be a bit pricey too. Consider, too that with a DJ, you'll also have an emcee to move the reception along.

We suggest you shop around extensively when looking for a DJ. Consider calling a local college to see if they can recommend a talented TV/R major who might be willing to take the job.

When picking out music, make sure you take into consideration the guests. An all-rap repertoire probably isn't appropriate, but all big band music isn't either. Make sure there's a mix of both to please both young and old.

To encourage guests to dance, assign each table a love song, when the band (or DJ) plays that song that table should get up to dance. You know likely know whether this would work or not with your crowd, but is a neat idea.

To be honest, really a very small percentage of the human race enjoys the Chicken Dance, Macarena, and Electric Slide. Know your guests, and if you know this will be uncomfortable for them, make sure your DJ does not include them. They can be embarrassing, but they can be great fun as well. It's truly a matter of preference!

If your hearts are set on live music, look for bands that have day jobs and "jam" for fun. Don't rule out high school-aged bands. Or hire a child violin virtuoso to perform for the ceremony -- there won't be a dry eye in the place.

Also, consider the time of your reception. My first wedding was held at 11:00 in the morning. The music at the reception was set to begin at 2:00 and we expected to be finished with the whole reception by 6:00. We had a favorite local band we loved and asked if they would cut their price for an afternoon "gig" since they would still be free to perform that evening. They were happy to and we got them for just $200. They got their regular bar rate that night and made a little extra on the side.

A rock-bottom budget option is to make your own tapes of your musical favorites. If you know of someone who has an awesome stereo system, see if they would be willing to loan it to you for the day and have people volunteer to man it to make sure you don't have any silent times.

The good part about mix CD's is that if you take some time, you can put it together so that it plays straight through and no one will have to switch discs. You can mix it up with an equal balance of fast and slow songs and add in all your favorites as well.

Another fun option for music is to have a karaoke set- up. You can maximize on the talents of some of your guests and laugh at the not-so-great talents of others. Some people really come to life with karaoke, you may as well maximize on that!

If you don't own a karaoke machine or know someone who does, look into renting one. You can download karaoke songs (music without the lyrics) online to make your own karaoke CD's. Go to lyrics.com to get the words and arrange it all in a simple 3-ring binder for your guests to refer to.

There are a lot of other miscellaneous ways to save money on your wedding. The next section covers some of these tips.

MISCELLANEOUS

Wedding Rings:

Wedding rings symbolize the union of two people joined by the ring finger. Some people say the ring finger has an artery that leads straight to the heart. I don't know if that's true but it is romantic.

Once married most people don't take off their wedding bands, as a sign of their faithfulness to each other. It's also a good idea to leave them on because it is surprisingly easy to lose your rings.

Here is the buzz on saving a few bucks on your wedding rings:

- Simple gold bands are the cheapest. They can run $125 to $400 each. They are also classic and elegant.

- Silver bands are modern and cheap.

- Don't buy the designer version of gold bands. That will save you a bunch.

- If you want white metal, opt for white gold. Platinum is almost double the price.

- You'll save almost half if you buy a coordinating set or trio (engagement ring, your wedding band and his band.)

- If you want a ring with a stone, don't forget semi-precious stones are beautiful. You don't have to have diamonds in your wedding rings.

- Family wedding bands are a romantic heirloom and free.

- Shopping online can save you money. Make sure you pick a secure site with great customer service.

- Check out local pawn shops too.

- Consider stones other than diamonds. Princess Diana had a sapphire ring, you could too!

- If you really want something more-make a plan-start saving now and decide to upgrade your wedding rings on your fifth anniversary or your tenth anniversary. Maybe you could plan to renew your vows then too!

Attendant Gifts:

For the girls, go practical. Buy pantyhose and a pretty necklace to wear at the wedding. You can often find strands of faux pearls cheaply in a jewelry shop like Claire's. If you get a really good deal, pop for earrings too!

For the guys, a money clip can run from $5.00 to $10.00 depending on where you look. Try Dollar General. You can even start them off with a dollar bill in it if you get them cheap enough.

The flower girl would probably love a stuffed animal.

Maybe a set of bears dressed in bride and groom attire. Since the flower girl and ring bearer are the youngest members of the wedding party, you may want to throw practicality out the door and just buy them a toy you know they'll love.

If you want to get creative, consider making each of your bridesmaids a photo collage or a small scrapbook with photos of you and them together. Small photo albums can be found at the dollar store and it takes just a glue gun and some imagination to decorate.

You can buy each attendant a book picked out especially for them. Write a personal inscription in the front of it. Gift certificates are also usually good gifts.

Consider also making your own bath products to give as gifts. Bath salts and soaps are actually quite easy and inexpensive to make. Recipes and directions can be found online or at the local craft store.

The Honeymoon:

Unless you have a rich relative who's willing to send you on a honeymoon cruise, a lavish honeymoon is probably out of the realm of possibility. But that doesn't mean you can't have a nice getaway after your wedding.

Consider local travel. Stay at a bed and breakfast.

What about a theme park honeymoon? Some couples relish the idea of camping. Rent and RV and get to an RV park for a secluded honeymoon where you can enjoy each other exclusively.

If you can get away for your honeymoon, be sure to plan early. The earlier you book your trip, the better chance you have of getting a good rate. Consider an all-inclusive vacation or a cruise. These can be relatively low-cost and immensely enjoyable!

Don't be afraid to ask for freebies. Everyone loves newlyweds, so take advantage of this nearly universal sentimentality by asking for discounts or freebies, suggests Ingram. If you tell your waiter that you're on your honeymoon, you may get a free dessert or bottle of wine.

Ask the desk clerk at the hotel where you're staying for any free upgrades, as well.

IN GENERAL

- Make a list of your dreams and prioritize them. Do the important things first.

- Purchase shoes, hose, undergarments, etc., that you can use for work after the wedding.

- Plan ahead, and do as much as you can yourself...but make sure the week of your wedding is free to relax and rest, so you can be at your best for the big day.

- For out of town guests, negotiate with a local hotel for a flat, group rate. Ask that the rate extend to a day or two before and after your wedding. Ask for group parking discounts too.

- Rent a Cadillac or other luxury vehicle just for the Bride, Groom, Maid/Matron of Honor, and Best Man to save on the expense of a limousine. The other members of the Bridal Party will most likely want to ride with their spouse, boyfriend or girlfriend to the reception.

- Kids can get bored during the wedding reception. So instead of having kids seated at the same table with the adults, you can have an area where kids can be more casual and can have a small party of their own.

- Instead of the traditional guest book, have a framed canvas for your guest to sign. This is something you can hang in your home as a unique memory of your wedding day. Leave blank squares to mount snap shots, from the ceremony to make as a collage.

- Marriage is a union of families. During the wedding rites, if possible, you may alter some of the practices to include the children of the bride or groom from previous marriage or the parents and families of the couple. Having them perform a special union rite will signify that the wedding is not just a union of two people but also of two families.

We did this in my second marriage. I have two children from my previous marriage and wanted to have them included in the ceremony. After my husband and I said our vows, we recited a separate set of vows to them promising to be loving parents and a happy family – in good times and bad. We've certainly had both!

After we said vows to them, my husband presented my daughter with her own "wedding ring" – a simple gold band with a small stone – and my son with a cross necklace. They loved it and it really united us as a family.

- When the bride and groom come out of the church, it is tradition to shower them with something. This tradition relates to wishing fertility on them in their marriage.

Traditionally, they have been showered with rice (uncooked, of course!) More and more people have gone toward bird seed which is more environmentally friendly. And no, birds won't explode if they eat the rice!

Another great idea besides rice or bird seed is to have the guests hold sparklers as the newlyweds exit the ceremony.

- Make sure any speeches are given early on in the reception. The longer the reception lasts, the more possibility of having an intoxicated, and probably inappropriate, toast!

- If you want an outdoor wedding, have a back-up plan in case of inclement weather.

- Rent, borrow, or make as many items as possible! Some items to borrow from a friend or relative are a cake knife and serving set, toasting glasses, jewelry and the bride's shoes. To reduce costs, you can make several items or enlist a few friends to help you with ribbons, pew bows, veil and headpiece, church programs, bridesmaids' dresses, bridal purse, ring bearer pillow and the cake topper.

- Though we've said it before, it bears repeating. Forget the "W" Word. While I have noticed a small change in recent years, this still holds true for a lot of cases.

People expect weddings to be more expensive, and are charged accordingly. Refer to your wedding as a family get-together or a gathering. It's unfortunate, but when you associate an item with a wedding, you will often find that the price goes up.

- Tulle can be a fairly inexpensive decorating tool (no pun intended). Tulle can be draped along staircases, balconies and fireplaces. Tulle bows can be tied around chairs. Some reception locations may not have the most "attractive" chairs. The tulle bows look beautiful and romantic and make a great "cover-up".

- Consider keeping the theme of your wedding and reception all the way into the restrooms! For example, if your theme is daisies then cut a few daisy heads off and lay them around the sinks. Perhaps you also might add soap and lotion for your guests to use that have the same scent as your wedding flowers.

- You will have to pay the officiant, so budget this into your expenses.

- The rehearsal dinner is traditionally given by the groom's family. But let's face it, sometimes tradition can go out the door in the best interest of the couple.

The rehearsal dinner of today doesn't have to be a formal sit-down dinner. More and more couples are opting for casual, simple get-togethers on the day before their marriage.

You can gather at someone's house and order pizza to eat while you socialize. You could also get sub sandwiches from the local sub shop.

Maybe simple pot luck would suffice for you. Why not put out some lunch meat and cheese for sandwiches?

Remember, you'll be stressed enough the next day, so relax on rehearsal night!

Here are the checklists we promised! Print them out and refer to them often. They can help keep you organized and insure that you have a beautiful wedding with no detail left untouched!

CONCLUSION

Weddings should reflect the individual personalities and priorities of the couple getting married. The focus of this special day need not be about how much was spent or saved. It should be about the event itself and the couple's commitment to each other.

Remember, it's not the price of the wedding that determines the quality of your marriage or that dictates a good time for all involved!

A successful wedding does not have to be an expensive wedding. Success should be determined by whether the bride, groom and the guests enjoyed themselves.

Having a wedding on a tight budget does not mean having to give up style or the fond memories. It just takes some planning and shopping around.

No matter how much money you spend, if your wedding is cookie cutter and seems rehearsed no one will remember it and most will not enjoy it. Make it your own, make it part of you both, not part of a book you read, or do things you think you "have" to do! Share with your guests part of who you both are!

Weddings are expensive if you want them to be. But if you want to keep money aside for a deposit on a house or a honeymoon to remember, then there are many cost cutting ideas. All you need is a little imagination, and some help from friends and family and you too can have a luxury wedding with all the trimmings.

Getting married should not be expensive. After all, the essence of marriage is in the union and not in the celebration. You shouldn't also try too hard to please the guests. Your family and friends are there to rejoice this wonderful event with you and not to criticize your wedding.

Think of your wedding as a collaboration of loving hands coming together to form the perfect day. Follow these tips and you'll have a beautiful wedding and reception and you won't have to start out married life in debt. You'll have a gorgeous and memorable ceremony to remember for years to come!

·

9 786069 837382

Printed by Libri Plureos GmbH in Hamburg,
Germany